Attitude
OVERHAUL

8 Steps To Win the War
On Negative Self-Talk

How to Use The Power of Your Mind To
Gain Confidence, Double Your Income,
And Find Life-Changing Love

KYLE ZDROIK

Attitude Overhaul: 8 Steps to Win the War on Negative Self-Talk

Copyright © 2010 by Kyle Zdroik

TABLE OF CONTENTS

INTRODUCTION

In today's world, having the "right" attitude is harder to understand than ever. What does attitude even mean? Think about the last time you said to yourself, "that person has an *attitude*". This person rushes to conclusions, doesn't take time to listen, and isn't willing to forgive. How do you maintain productivity at work and home when your co-worker or partner drowns you out? Now, turn the mirror back at yourself. Have you ever thought about how others perceive your attitude? Have you ever been told that your attitude has affected the outcome of a promotion, or even a relationship?

Attitude Overhaul was designed to help you identify your own attitude by using a self-discovery approach, packaged in an easier-than-ever way for you to develop an understanding of your own attitude.

As a young professional and lifetime optimist, I found that attitude truly does make the difference. Working in sales, I've been around hundreds of customers, made thousands of phone calls, and have been in and out of multiple relationships. Each of these experiences has helped me discover something new about my own attitude.

So many entrepreneurs, students, mothers, fathers, and young professionals have struggled to put their finger on why they do what they do, where their thoughts come from, why they believe what they believe, and why their results never seem to change. That is why implementing these easy-to-follow steps will lead you to the discovery of your own attitude. If you feel like you have an understanding, the steps in this book will allow you to develop a better awareness of where the messages in your self-talk are coming from.

While pursuing my bachelor's degree, I've always had a burning desire to help others. Once a professor told me I was a "natural teacher and motivator". It was those kind words that inspired me to give, write, and share this book with you today.

I developed this program by pulling together certain experiences in my life that have helped me to create a better understanding of my own attitude. The steps I lay out for you in this book are the same principles I've applied to my own life. The results have been incredible; through the implementation of this altered mindset, in nearly one year, I have doubled my income (nearly quadrupling my sales), asked the woman of my dreams to be my wife, and bought my first home.

I promise that if you follow this step-by-step book, you will be able to become a person that you identify as financially successful, and one that flourishes in relationships with friends and family. Once you understand why you have made the choices in your life thus far, I can show you how to maintain the discipline to gain the new results you desire.

Don't be the person who goes back in to work on Monday asking yourself the same questions you left Friday with. Why haven't I gotten a raise? Why hasn't that customer bought from me yet? Why aren't the relationships in my life as successful as I'd like them to be? Don't be that person. Take this opportunity to follow my step-by-step program and become the person that others perceive as positive, outgoing, energetic, enthusiastic, and encouraging to others.

I must warn you, change is a challenge; however, pushing yourself outside your comfort zone will open up doors to new opportunities. It is essential to first understand your own attitude before you can blame others for the environment you currently live in today.

Well, what do you say? Let's get started!

CHAPTER 1

Step 1:
What does <u>Attitude</u>
Mean to You?

I first want to take a minute to say thank you for taking the time to invest in yourself! This book is going to be amazing, providing you with a unique opportunity to understand your internal mindset, which is ultimately responsible for the attitude you display. My hope is that each step will allow you to gain insight to why certain events have occurred, or may not have occurred, in your life.

Determine Good Attitude vs. Bad Attitude.

One thing is for certain: We all have a lot of thoughts and ideas that are continually being processed by our brains. Often, we don't understand where they are coming from or who is influencing them.

Your Mind is the Battleground

When self-talk takes place, the battle for your energy commences. Your mind is the battleground between two opponents: positive and negative emotions. In many instances, it is challenging to put a finger on exactly where an emotion came from. The opponents have several different attributes and qualities that make them unique. The strength of an individual's positive or negative attitude varies from person to person depending on which opponent is more trained and disciplined for success.

Before you make any assumptions about which team (positive or negative) is stronger for you personally, you need to define a representation of Positive Attitude and Negative Attitude. Each person visualizes situations through their own paradigm, which is created through the perspectives you share with those that are closest to you. In general, a person's outlook and mindset is determined by those he or she is surrounded by.

To begin, let's discover what is happening on your personal mind battleground.

Reflect by answering a few questions:

- Why do I behave the way I do?

- Why do I feel certain emotions?

- Why do I react the same way to a specific person every time I see him/her?

- Why do I always seem to get the same results?

These are good questions to ask yourself to expand your understanding of why you feel and react a certain way in various situations. These thoughts don't come from something that happened today; they were developed over time and through experiences.

More often than not, your intuition evolved from prior interactions with your family, a relationship, or an observation of a close friend's experience. For example, while working out at your local fitness facility, you had a negative encounter with another member who made a comment about your body weight. If you began your day in negative state, it would be easy to yell, scream, and become defensive during your next personal interaction. Now, if you were confident in your own skin and had experience challenging predispositions, a comment like this would roll right off. You wouldn't think much of it!

Challenge Your Thinking

Predispositions play a large part in what attitude means to you, both in current and previous situations. Your brain accesses stored data you've gathered during your life, to assist in determining how you perceive each situation. In the future, when you experience a similar situation, the brain will expedite this determination process, reacting in a similar fashion. This will continue to occur if your perception isn't threatened with a new positive outlook, making it almost impossible to break your negative habits. Don't allow your brain to give in to negativity; challenge it!

Your attitude has been shaped from a young age through the morals and values your parents raised you to believe as truth. It is likely that if your mother had a PhD in Biochemistry from Harvard University, and your father had a Finance degree from Wharton School of Finance, you view attaining educational success as a positive behavior. In this case, your parents would likely place a high value on education, as they were able to better their lives because of it. To the contrary, if you were raised in poverty and your parents only attained high school diplomas, you may not see the value in a college education.

Now that you have an understanding of where some of your thoughts, attitudes, and actions may have originated, let's spend some time discussing the mindset of Positive Attitude. Please understand that the qualities I share will be particular to myself. You may find as I explain a few of these, you don't fully identify with them. That is totally okay! I will help lay the foundation, allowing you to identify which qualities best fit into your Positive Attitude Paradigm.

Positive Attitude Mindset: Happiness, Persistence, and Momentum

- **Happiness:** Happiness is different to each person. That's why I have asked you to identify certain aspects of what composes your attitude as a whole (Positive and Negative). You are responsible for creating your own happiness. Below, I will share with you a few items to assist in the expansion of your Positive Attitude mindset:

  ✓ *Always be in pursuit of your goals* - Focus on the goals that get you excited. Fall in love with the thought of accomplishing your most audacious goals, literally to the point where you become obsessed with achieving them. Be creative on a continuous basis, always be willing to adjust to life, and find ways to breathe life into the possibilities! Keep your eyes on the prize. This will keep you motivated, even when times are tough.

  ✓ *Have the guts to say "Yes"* - Some of the most pessimistic people you will meet in your life are filled with fear and doubt. They will be the first to reach out to you, willing to justify why a new opportunity in your life will fail. This is due to feelings of discomfort with stepping out of their own comfort zone to achieve their full potential. They are unable to try something challenging due to the chance of failure. Be willing to fail. Mention to your pessimistic friends that you appreciate their experience, but you are going to go for it any way!

✓ *Your mind is only as capable as your body allows* - Fundamentally, this is one of the simplest concepts to live by. However, in nearly every personal growth book you will read, it never receives enough attention. My experience has always been that you must take care of your body through regular physical activity, fitness, and a healthy lifestyle to have a fit mindset.

✓ Exercise, in my mind, is the most beneficial; increasing your daily energy allows your mind to function at a higher level. However, most people do not understand this essential connection between the mind and body, neglecting exercise due to busy schedules.

✓ Eat right! Do not allow processed foods and complex carbohydrates to fill your shopping cart due to the reduced prices and convenience. Budget your finances to allow for expenditure on whole, minimally processed food. Think about this as an investment in your future, potentially reducing health conditions, complications, medications, medical bills, and allowing you to live a longer, active, and independent lifestyle.

✓ Sleep. Turn back the clock to the last experience you had with minimal hours of sleep. It is likely that it wasn't very easy to find the best in every situation, or function at your full potential.

✓ *Smile early and often* - As I mentioned earlier, happiness is intentional and so is smiling. Always be looking for situations to smile and share your positivity and happiness with the world. Remember, the more you give, the more you will receive. In my experience, smiling has a nice "boomerang" effect, attracting positive, happy people back to your life! Smile so much that it becomes an involuntary behavior, like breathing, that your body starts doing naturally. Trust me, this alone could dramatically attract better results to your life. Customers, friends, and family like to be with people that are happy. Smiling displays confidence. Confidence makes people feel safe. When people feel safe, trust is built!

• **Persistence:** Persistence is key. It will be necessary for qualities of a Positive Attitude mindset to assist you in small daily victories as well as some longer lifelong battles against negativity. After you make the decision to challenge your predispositions, your Negative Attitude mindset begins to abate and diminish. Never forget how poorly you felt when you gave in and lost to Negative Attitude.

✓ I learned this at a young age, during my first career in direct marketing. I had a goal to make 100 phone calls on a Sunday morning. However, when my friends asked me to go out on a Saturday night and stay up late, I seemed to let my sales goals take a back seat. Remember, your close friends will always stand by your side (even if you miss one Saturday night with them out on the town). Needless to say, I didn't make it into the office on Sunday, thus my sales goal wasn't met. Have the gull and willingness to persist in achieving your goals. It is remembering those experiences that will drive you to make better decisions in the future!

• **Momentum:** Endurance and practice of a positive mindset will create valuable momentum in your life. A Negative Attitude mindset will always be strong and influential, wanting you to succumb to "easy" choices. Challenge these Negative Attitude thoughts through the use of happiness and persistence. Eventually, you will become disgusted with the outcomes of choices swayed by negativity. With the consistent use of positive attitude, momentum will help you achieve a new level of success that you've never experienced before.

✓ This quality will be supported by the positive results and feedback you will be given along your journey. I remember this was never more evident than when I had a sales goal to sell $10,000 worth of product in a 14 day time period. Starting out the sales competition, I had a positive mindset, that results were destined to come my way. However, the results did not initially come as I had planned. When I was at only $5,000 in sales by day 10, my positivity and momentum stalled. I had to be strong-willed at this moment, keeping my goal in mind, and remember why I was working so hard to achieve my goal. On day 11, I received the largest order of my career, selling $2,357 worth of product!

✓ This put me back in the driver's seat to achieving my goal of $10,000. That day, everything seemed to change. Customers started answering my calls, each one would offer to give me 15 recommendations, and I was selling on each appointment. The momentum was back! Remember to always keep a positive mindset and trust the results will follow.

At this point, you're probably wondering, "How do I know if I have felt positive momentum?"

I challenge you to think about your experiences you have had during, what you consider, your best job so far.

- How did you treat others?

- How did your co-workers treat you?

- Were you able learn and acquire skills in a faster manner?

Momentum is Key to Success and Growth

"When you're that successful, things have a momentum, and at a certain point you can't really tell whether you have created the momentum or it's creating you."

- Annie Lennox

It is likely that while working at your favorite job, you had built momentum, which helped to weaken and defeat Negative Attitude. During this time, it may have been easier to direct your attitude; allowing you the ability to respond in a better light even in unfavorable circumstances. Developing this type of momentum will play a large role in how your attitude paradigm is shaped in all situations moving forward.

It is also equally important to develop an understanding of the components that make up Negative Attitude.

Negative Attitude Mindset: Anger, Rudeness, and Slander

- **Anger:** Anger will often appear as a result of a situation or circumstance that is not going in your favor and can present itself daily if you let it go "unchecked". An example of this would be dealing with young children. It takes time and practice for a child to develop fundamental physical, social, and mental skills, which can, at times, strain a person's patience. For example, if you are in a rush to get to work and your child is having trouble tying their shoes, this may promote you to become irritated. This can lead to anger if the child continually doesn't perform the task at a pace to your expectations. For yourself, tying a shoe comes so easily you don't even have to think about it. It is almost subconscious. However, for a growing child, they are gaining fine motor skills and the ability to perform multi-step tasks, so tying a shoe isn't second nature to them. It is very important to see these situations through the eyes of others and check yourself. Thus, a person's patience and perspective go hand in hand when determining their attitude and reactions to others. Reacting with anger never works out. You look like a jerk, and it may greatly impact relationships with co-workers or those you love the most, such as friends and family.

- **Rudeness:** This is a behavior often promoted by Negative Attitude when it is hard to hear out another person's differing opinion to your own. Often, most people that are considered "rude" display behaviors that aren't well thought out. They tend to be selfish in nature, meaning they will say the first thing that comes to mind, without thinking about how the other person may feel or react. Regardless of the situation, never allow this behavior to become a part of who you are as a person. Being "rude" effectively is the same as sharing communication poison with your friends and family.

- **Slander:** This is a typical behavior Negative Attitude will persuade you to use when you are jealous. Maybe you believe that you should have received something that another person did. For example, a co-worker with a similar resume and qualifications gets promoted over you. Don't spread gossip or belittle them. Gossip has a boomerang effect; what goes around comes back around. You should expect that if you talk poorly about someone they're probably doing it back to you. If you are planning to continue working at that job or using co-workers as references for a new job, avoid slander. Live your life with optimism and an attitude that creates behavior allowing you to reap the benefits of positive results.

Now that you have an understanding of some of the characteristics that define positive and negative attitudes, it's time to determine what it all means. In the first step of this process, I wanted to share with you the basics of how I visualize attitude (to start at a very surface level). I believe most of the thoughts you have today are from beliefs shared from the perspective of your family. Next, I'll challenge your perception of attitude that was shaped based on the behaviors of your closest friends.

Your current attitudinal perspective wasn't developed overnight. Your perspective wasn't created exclusively by your family either. In the next section of step one, I'm going to speak about five parts that make up your current attitude philosophy. These five parts are people; the people that play the most influential part in the development of both your Positive and Negative Attitudes.

Do I Challenge the Thoughts My Friends Share with Me?

In developing a positive attitude is important to you take a close look at your friends.

I challenge you to pick up your phone right now.

Take a look at the last five people you have texted or called. Do those people possess some of the positive characteristics we discussed earlier? Are they genuine, caring, and happy? Are they willing to help others or help you create positive contagious momentum in your life? Believe it or not, you are letting these people greatly influence your attitude and perspective each day. By giving them your time and attention through phone or text, you are handing them a small key to influence in your life.

I understand every situation is a bit different. However, it is very important to be willing to spend less time with the people that are detractors of Positive Attitude (qualities that are loved by the negative attitude) and more time with those that help create the version of you that is desired!

In Step 1, we discussed the fact that your mind is truly a battleground. On a daily basis, there is a fight between positive and negative attitude. I shared with you some of the characteristics I feel compose both a positive and negative attitude, and how important it is to starve and deplete the Negative Attitude.

At this point, you understand that your current attitudinal paradigm has been greatly influenced by how you and your family perceive each situation. You also have identified the top five friends you are in most contact with, who are playing a large role influencing the choices you make in your life.

In order to graduate to Step 2, you need to look internally on your definitions of Positive and Negative Attitude. I now want you to identify what your own attitude means to you.

Action: Write your name in the middle of a blank sheet of paper and circle it.

- Next, draw a line from your name connecting it to another circle and label this circle "Positive Attitude". Under that Positive Attitude circle, write down every positive attitude trait you believe you possess with connecting lines. For example: Kindness, Energy, Encouragement, Respect, Helping, and Optimism.

- Go back to the center circle with your name in it. Now draw another circle branching off with the label "Negative Attitude". As with the list of positive attitude characteristics, write down every negative attitude trait you feel you possess. For example: Rude, Yelling, Gossip, and Anger. Be honest with yourself.

- Now, for a couple of your characteristics from both the positive and negative circles, try and come up with a specific example of how you demonstrated either a Positive or Negative Attitude. For example: "Positive Attitude" – Helping – "I helped Mary at work today. She was behind on her goals and I helped her catch up." A Negative Attitude example may look as such: "Negative Attitude" – Rude – "Yesterday, I was getting off of the elevator at work, was in a hurry, and didn't hold the door open for someone who asked me to hold it for them."

- Set a timer for 5 minutes to complete this exercise. Even if you don't share a specific written example for

each, take a moment to debrief on each attitude quality
you identified with yourself.

Example

Negative
Attitude

Rude   Short
Yelling Anger

Positive
Attitude

Hapiness   Helping
Persistence Loving

Specific Rude Behavior:

Yesterday, I was getting of
the elevator at work, was in
a hurry, and didn't hold the
door for someone who
asked me to hold it for them.

Specific Helping Behavior:

I helped Mary at work today.
She was behind in her goals
and I helped her catch up.

CHAPTER 2

Step 2:
Who is Fighting on Your Negative Attitude Side?

Awesome work! You have completed the first step of winning the war of the mind. By completing the first step, you have developed a better understanding of what you believe attitude is, how it's developed, what it consists of, and who continually influences it.

In the second step, we are going to "dig deeper" into analyzing Negative Attitude. I will refer to the top five Negative Attitudes (we will be calling them "warriors") known as the "Fearful Five". I will spend time discussing each of these in depth, as well as the qualities each of them promote in the mind.

To begin the second step, the only thing you need to know is that you must win the war. It is that simple, and is the only option. Often times, people associate negative thoughts with the word, war; however, in this case I must, for the repercussion of a poor attitude can be severe.

In order to win the war, you have to give conscious attention to the army that is fighting the battle against you. The negative attitude side has many different options; people and products that are trying to defeat you every day! Each person reading this is a little bit different in what influences him or her. That is why conscious effort is important.

Positive Attitude Warriors

These are the good guys. It is important to keep these warriors strong, well fed, and properly nourished. They are going to stand up against the negative attitude warriors that are constantly invading your mind every day. For example, if you are reading this book fully energized, optimistic, and open-minded with an understanding of what you want out of life, your positive attitude warriors will prevail.

Negative Attitude Warriors

These are the bad guys. Ideally, you'll want to make sure you keep these warriors malnourished and give them as little time and attention as possible. They are trying to seize all of your time and energy. At the same time, they will eradicate your positive habits, leaving them fragile and exhausted. For example, at this moment, if you are a little bit tired or lacking energy, it is because the opposition is sucking up all of your energy and passion.

The "Fearful Five" Warriors of the Negative Attitude:

Media Monger ⤳

Let's take a look at the first of the Fearful Five known as the "Media Monger".

This warrior is known to use the media to infiltrate your thoughts.

The "Media Monger" promotes the following characteristics:

- Misconceptions
- False Reality
- Violence
- Anger

Each time you turn on the news, the "Media Monger" puts on his gear and goes to work on your mind. He rings the doorbell for access every day around 5:00 pm, right after you get home from work. You graciously open the door, pressing the power button on your remote, granting him unlimited access. He is immediately hitting you with negative experiences the world has for that day, fighting your positive attitude presenting every shooting, murder, stabbing, rape, homicide, political slandering, budget deficit, unemployment rate, and stock decline to influence your thoughts. For him, this is easy. It is 5:00 pm, and your positive attitude characteristics are at their most vulnerable time, taking a rest.

Why does this happen? The answer is quite simple actually. Think about all of the conversations you have with your best friend or spouse. I would assume it is probably easier to slander someone you know than to spend time giving credit to a co-worker or relative that is doing well. In the minds of most, media compartmentalizes itself to be known as fact. They can pull information from Facebook, Twitter, and Instagram to find out what is getting the most "Likes", "Retweets", and what is "Trending". This fills our mind with negative information, due to the fact it is popular amongst the majority of people. This warrior understands that most are losing the battle of the mind; losing their own wars against Negative Attitude.

Let's face it. If junk TV is what catches people's attention, they are going to put it on the news. They need to get ratings, ratings equal more advertising dollars, and more advertising dollars equals more revenue to the news company. I want you to look at the news like donuts are to food. Donuts are very easy to eat, but we don't eat them every day because we know if we did it would negatively affect our health and deprive our body of important nutrients/vitamins that we attain from healthier food options. This is the same thing mentally that will happen to your mind if you fill it with the news each night.

> "I find television very educating. Every time somebody turns on the set, I go into the other room and read a book."

— Groucho Marx

The media is patient. It takes the necessary time to build up our knowledge on issues that are taking place worldwide. Using the base layer of knowledge they share with you, they are able to significantly influence the way that we view certain issues.

If not confronted, this warrior will play a significant role in your life experience. This is never more evident than when we look at the life of a teenager. They will watch TV shows filled with love, relationships, fashion, and violence. If the beliefs they consume from the media aren't challenged by Positive Attitude, Negative Attitude will take every opportunity to try and control your behavior to mirror what you view on TV.

I believe people live with good intentions, I do. However, don't you think if people were really intrigued by how many leaders were promoted and animals saved from torture, that the media would play that full time between the hours of 5:00 pm and midnight? The truth is, most people aren't making a conscious effort to fight their own war on Negative Attitude. The "Media Monger" is winning when the media is winning, defeating minds, and controlling people's lives by influencing the actions they take and the way they talk.

The "Media Monger" is best fought off with discipline. One needs to have the self-discipline to recognize that watching TV for hours after work isn't moving his/her lives forward in a positive direction. Be conscious of the alternative choices you could make with that time. Consider the following potential examples:

- Choose to go watch your son or daughter at their away basketball game instead of watching TV after work.

- Choose to have a deep conversation for the first time in months with your significant other.

- Choose to begin working on yourself, developing your skills after work to become a more valuable person in your position at work.

If you make the choice and challenge the "Media Monger", it can be defeated over time. Use your awareness, and make the right choices with your time. Put yourself in the best position to succeed both at work and home. It is those that are unaware or not willing to challenge their choices of time after work that the "Media Monger" will feed off.

Raging Recruiter

The next warrior of the "Fearful Five" on the negative attitude side is known as the "Raging Recruiter".

The "Raging Recruiter" promotes the following characteristics:

- Slander
- Libel
- False Information
- Gossip

He possesses the qualities of promotion, infiltrating your mind with negative ideas. You have probably experienced situations in your professional career where the Negative Attitude side uses the "Raging Recruiter". Be candid with yourself when you go speak with a co-worker about another co-worker that was promoted quicker than both of you. Even if he or she has worked in the same position for a significantly less period of time, is the conversation often more positive or negative?

Please correct me if I'm wrong. Do the following lines sound familiar?

Susan: "Greg has been with the company for two years and was promoted to account technician II. I've been with the company for ten years and I'm still at level I. How is that possible?"

Bill: "Yeah, Greg works hard, but I agree with you. It is unacceptable. I can't believe Tom (the supervisor) would pick him for the promotion!"

Susan: "I see how this company operates. I guess you need to be a part of the 'boys club' to be promoted around here."

Bill: "I completely agree. I wonder what Tom was thinking. Maybe you should go talk to him and tell him how you are feeling."

Susan: "Nah, I don't think so. Besides, how is that going to help? That isn't going to change anything. My friend Beth over at ABC Wireless is hiring. Would you be interested in moving companies with me if I left?"

In this scenario, Susan has brought Bill to the water cooler. Susan has worked years for this company and hasn't been promoted, likely hasn't had a conversation with Tom, and will continue to slander his decision-making in the future. The "Raging Recruiter" loves recruiting someone like Bill. They don't take responsibility for their own results, likely live paycheck to paycheck, and play the blame game any chance they get to justify poor results.

The "Raging Recruiter" is best fought off by the positive attitude, from a warrior who possesses the skill of curiosity and responsibility. An individual needs to have the mindset to consider, "Maybe this happened because..." This ignites the curiosity mindset to discover a positive reason as to why another is doing well.

Let's take a look at how this situation would be handled by Susan and Bill if they were both aware of the "Recruiter" attempting to take over their thoughts and actions. You'll see in this next situation how things would have played out if Susan had taken responsibility for her results.

Susan: "Greg has been with the company for two years and was promoted to account technician II. I've been with the company for ten years and I'm still at level I. How is that possible?"

Bill: "I completely understand the way you feel, Susan. It took me nearly seven years to get my first promotion working for Tom. However, with Greg, **maybe this happened because** he shows up on time every day, always has positive things to say about the people around him, and has met some very tight deadlines."

Susan: "Yeah, I guess I never looked at it that way. I have missed some deadlines over the years, and came in late on a couple of days I had projects due. He has always been nice to me, and actually helped me learn new skills at my current position."

Bill: "Maybe it would be best to congratulate Greg on his promotion and find out how he earned it."

Susan: "Well, I want to get promoted, so yes, that sounds like a great idea. Let's head back over there."

In this situation, Susan uses the best ammunition within to fight off the "Raging Recruiter": taking responsibility. She took responsibility for her previous actions that may have led to less than favorable results, such as not getting a promotion. She went on to admit that Greg does possess some favorable qualities that have lifted up the entire team since he has come on board. She finished off with a compliment of Greg's skills, sharing with Bill that she too has learned to become better at her job because of Greg.

Admission, self-reflection, and happiness were the three key qualities used effectively in the most recent scenario to win this battle. Susan took responsibility and thought differently after Bill shared with her a different way to look at the situation; this is very hard to do! We all want to rush to defend our actions and blame others or circumstances for our poor results. Really think about this point for a moment. If tomorrow you were the CEO of your company and were asked to develop a company that was highly profitable and filled with talent, would you promote yourself? You would likely promote someone that is outperforming their pay grade. Someone who helps recruit others to do well. Someone who brings a high level of value to the organization you run!

Worry Wart

Staring at you from a distance in your brain is the next contender on the battleground, known as the "Worry Wart".

The "Worry Wart" promotes the following characteristics:

- Worry
- Self-Doubt
- Limiting Self-Worth
- Health, Financial, and Social Risk

Negative Attitude loves to use this warrior during times when you feel the most vulnerable; whether it is just coming off of a relationship break up, losing your biggest client, or finding out you lost a loved one in a car accident. The "Worry Wart" has a strength and ability to cause health, social, and family problems. He can be deadly if not addressed soon enough. Learn the skills to be a positive attitude warrior, not a worrier!

Three very well known prey of this warrior are a college student, sales person, and single parent. These three positions require attention in multiple facets of their lives.

For example, the sales person might get 30 payment delinquency e-mail notices of customers that didn't pay their bills on time. This is where the 'Worry' comes alive, trying to win the war of the mind right at that instance, immediately flooding your mind with doubt, and the wonder if your actions lead to the current situation. Did I not tell them to pay on the 15th of the month? Did I set up the wrong pay plan for this customer? Find the courage within to understand you can't control every situation.

The solution to defeating this is challenging the thought of losing sleep and waking up in the middle of the night thinking about situations that are out of your control. Kick the "Worry Wart" out of your mind by challenging him, scaring him away with confidence and the realization that you should only react emotionally to the results that happen in situations you can control. Get busy staying positive and influencing the results of situations you have control over. In my experience in sales, when I become worried with a situation I feel like I negatively impacted, I will seek clarity. Make a phone call. Find out the truth of the situation! Write down exactly what you are worried about, on paper. Then, make a call to your manager or boss to work through situations that can make you anxious.

Most situations you won't be able to control, such as the temperature, rain, or level of sunshine. What you can control is the way you react to the situation that was given to you that day, which was outside of your control.

> "Worry often gives a
> small thing a big shadow."
>
> – Swedish Proverb

Negative Nancy

Your next opponent is "Negative Nancy".

"Negative Nancy" promotes the following qualities:

- Pessimism
- Distrust
- Doubt
- Cynicism

Negative Attitude loves to use "Negative Nancy" during time you spend thinking big. These are the moments where you have your second cup of coffee in the morning and utter the words, "What if..."

- What if I was rich enough to buy a private jet?

- What if I was a good enough husband that my wife came home every day after work and said, "I love you"?

- What if I spent so much time educating my children they were able to get into an Ivy League school?

"Negative Nancy" will take that opportunity to penetrate your mind and fill it with doubt, making you question your optimistic moment. This warrior will make you feel defeated,

ATTITUDE OVERHAUL

thinking there is no way that your optimistic thought could ever happen. Then, she will fill your mind with reasons to back up the doubtful claim, bringing to the front of your mind all of the times you went to the edge of your comfort zone and failed. She will remind you of the last time you thought you could be something more than you are. The last time you risked it all.

This warrior came to fight against my positive attitude many times, but was never more evident than a couple years ago when I was considering a job promotion. Instantly, when I was presented with this great opportunity, "Negative Nancy" rushed in bringing back all the memories I had growing up where I risked it all and failed. She reminded me of how comfortable I am with my life in my current position, and by taking on a new opportunity, I could lose everything I had! This warrior is definitely one of the most difficult opponents I've had to face when making the decision to take on a new role within the company.

The best ammunition I had to fight off "Negative Nancy" was with the willingness to take a risk, and self-confidence in my abilities.

- When "Negative Nancy" comes knocking at the door of your mind, instantly find a pen and paper. Start writing your thoughts down on paper. Trust me, when you transfer your negative thoughts from your mind to paper, they become less terrifying.

- When I am in a situation in life where I know the "Negative Nancy" will show up, I meet it with reasons. If I have self-doubt about going out on a limb or taking a life risk, I will write down the answers I come up with to the following question:

"What are five reasons why this risk WILL work out?"

Once you come up with the five answers, write them down.

Second, read them out loud to yourself. Keep re-reading them until you are 100% convinced that it is possible to make even your most unrealistic dreams come true.

Pessimistic Peter

"Pessimistic Peter" is another opponent you will face. His primary potion is, and you guessed it, planting pessimism in the brain.

"Pessimistic Peter" loves to promote the following characteristics:

- Pessimism
- Self-Doubt
- Lack of Trust
- Reasons to Doubt

Negative Attitude loves to use "Pessimistic Peter" when you ask yourself the following questions:

- "I know last time I attempted college I dropped out. I wonder if I could make it all the way through if I went back?"

- "I know I have failed in my last two relationships, but I really like Beth. I wonder if this time it will work out?"

"Pessimistic Peter" will rush to fight, sharing past experiences you've had where things didn't work out. He makes you believe that you have no shot to accomplish your goals, flooding your brain with endless self-doubt. This leads you to believe that nothing has changed in your life to indicate the result will be different this time around.

The best ammunition to this is to use, well you guessed it, optimism. This is the greatest ammunition to defeat the Negative Attitude side because it destroys stories of the past. It opens the mental doors to new opportunity, not hanging on to past results to make future decisions. Trust yourself and believe that you can break a negative cycle. The fruit in life always seems to hang from the limbs of the longest branches.

You are now equipped with greater awareness of the opponents that you are going to face today, tomorrow, and the next day. You learned that the "Media Monger" is going to try to influence you with false reality. The "Raging Recruiter" is going to be that thought you have about a co-worker who shared with you some gossip he or she wants you to share with someone else, and wants you to hop on the bandwagon. The "Worry Wart" is going to do his best to fill your mind with worry and self-doubt, consistently flooding the mind with the thoughts of failed past experiences. "Negative Nancy" will hit you as soon as you have a thought about doing something you've never done before. And last but not least in the "Fearful Five" is "Pessimistic Peter". He is a lot like "Negative Nancy" in the sense that he will fill your mind with doubt when you are feeling optimistic.

Action: In order to complete step 2, you will write down, next to you and your top five friends, who you feel is being defeated by the "Media Monger", "Raging Recruiter", "Worry Wart", "Negative Nancy", and "Pessimistic Peter".

- Write their names below the portion of the paper you started in step 1. Simply write each of those opponents next to you and your top five friends' names and place a yes or no to each if you feel they are winning or losing to that opponent.

- After you have identified whom you feel is being defeated, next to each, briefly think about why you feel that way. For example, you might say, "My Dad is being defeated by the "Media Monger". Each day when he gets home from work, he kicks his feet up on the couch and watches TV until he goes to bed that evening."

- Once you have taken a moment to thoughtfully access the attitudes of those that are closest to you in your life, it is time to tally up your results. Above each person, put the score out of five that each of your friends received. In my example, each friend would receive a point for each "yes" they receive from you.

- This should only take a moment. Take your cell phone and set a timer for five minutes. This will allow you to stay focused and propel you to step 3.

39

Example

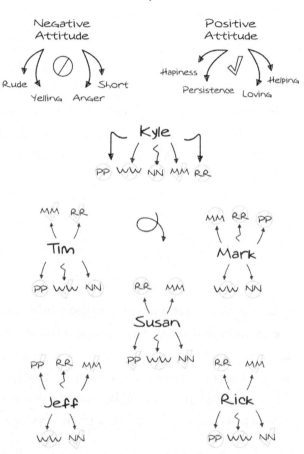

Kyle (Me) – 1/5

Top 5 Friends:

- Tim – 3/5

- Mark – 0/5

- Susan – 2/5

- Jeff – 3/5

- Rick – 2/5

In this activity, similar to golf, a lower score is a better score. So, in this example, according to the scoring criteria, Mark would be the friend of mine that I believe is currently winning the war against the "Fearful Five".

CHAPTER 3

Step 3:
Reflect on Who is
Influencing Your Decisions

Nice work! You have successfully completed the first two steps of developing a better understanding of which side is winning the battle of your thoughts. In the first step, you took a bit of time to gather a fresh perspective on Attitude and spent a little bit of time discovering what Attitude means to you. In the second step, we took a look at the five most influential warriors that are fighting for the Negative Attitude side.

In the third step, we are going to be taking a closer look at *how your friends play a role in terms of influencing your decisions.* You're going to be challenged when considering how each of your friends played a role in how you've become the person you are today. The first consideration I take in reflecting on my friends is their current career path.

- What do each of your five closest friends do for work?

In my opinion, your financial success will be based on the average of the five closest friends you have. Now, just because your closest friends aren't wealthy and you want to be rich, doesn't mean that they would be a bad friend. However, if you want to become a millionaire, you need to be looking for friends that are millionaires. Similarly, if you wanted to be a billionaire, you would need to find friends that are billionaires. You would pick up on the way they walk, talk with people, and handle themselves on a professional level.

Your friends are essentially mirrors to what your life looks at from a relational and financial level. I would be willing to bet that your current income is about the average amongst your top five friends.

Let's take, for example, Donald Trump. Do you believe he spends time around people that are in poverty? No. He is a billionaire and spends his time with others that are like him. If your friends aren't the reflection of who you want to be, you need to start seriously thinking about who you spend your time with. Who is influencing you? Value your time as much as diamonds. If your friends' values don't reflect the attitude you wish others to see in you, let them go. Now, I understand that there are circumstances, like a mother or father, you can't change. However, you should be putting in as much effort to head in the right direction as soon as possible.

In the introduction, I mentioned that through the process of applying the principles from this book, I was able to double my income. This was made possible by my friend Mark assisting me in shaping my way of thinking. After completing step two of this program, I find it quite fitting that he (in my opinion) would score the best in terms of defeating the "Fearful Five" in his own life. I appreciate Mark and his rich thinking. He has plenty of money, and pushed me to think bigger, go out on a limb, and take the risk of a job promotion.

I strongly believe that I am not alone in the situation I was in just over a year ago. I worked inside of a cubical, didn't see the growth or opportunity, and was there purely to pay my bills and nothing more. The money was the only thing that I could see; that is the only thing that kept me coming to work on a daily basis. I was convinced there had to be more opportunity, I knew I was worth more to the company. I used the skill of curiosity that my friend Mark has always taught me to use during times of doubt. Keep your eyes and ears open for new opportunities that might create a better freedom for both you and your family's future.

Recognizing that Mark shared the same financial goals that I did, I sought help from him. I shared with Mark that I was presented with a potential job opportunity at work. Mark asked me, "Does it align with your vision of the future?" That is an example of WINNING LANGUAGE! How powerful! This new job opportunity did align with the future I wanted to create for myself.

I shared with Mark that I was concerned and fearful to change jobs. I was at a job that had a consistent paycheck and was located in a part of the state where my friends and family lived. Mark told me that the best fruit is always at the end of the branch. He said, "Your true friends will never leave you. Opportunities like this don't always knock twice." It was the sense of security I craved, as I believe many do.

Security is a mindset used as an excuse many will use to not even attempt a walk down the wobbly branch of insecurity.

Now, almost 12 months later, I have gone from a job to a career. The career change has allowed me to double my income in one year! Boy, I'm glad that I took a walk down the branch of insecurity and believed in my abilities! This was all possible because I took on the risk that was necessary to take my income to the next level.

On the flip side is my friend Jeff. If presented with a new job offer, he would probably be the first person to side with security. Ever since high school, he has worked at my hometown gas station. He is a friend I've had for the longest time, but our attitudes and perspectives greatly differ. Jeff is never one to push himself to become better financially or relationally. He is known for taking advantage of every opportunity to blame the government or his personal upbringing for his financial short falls. LOSER TALK!

On the same level of importance as finances is the way each of your closest friends are in their personal relationships. Do you want to be defined as someone who is considered loyal and committed? Then, I would recommend picking up some of the ways that your friends winning the battle of the mind view their relationships. If one of your friends has been married for 10, 20 or 30 years, I'll bet that he or she has some great advice on maintaining good personal and most likely work relationships.

Which of your five friends have the best relationships with their spouse?

From a relationship level, friends like to hang out with other friends that are in relationships themselves. It's that simple. Single guys and girls like to hang out with others that are single because they can relate with one another. They are the people that will, more likely than not, validate their behaviors. Many times your internal desires don't match the behaviors that you are exhibiting in front of your friends.

You need to challenge your thinking! If you are single and would like to enter a relationship, it is going to take some level of risk on your part to become a reflection of your values. Muster up the courage to ask one of your closest friends about their experience with a successful relationship. Find out what they are doing. See if he or she can offer you any honest advice or feedback. This is how you will find life changing love in your personal and professional relationships!

In this step, the primary focus was on creating a clear understanding of how you feel about each of your friends in terms of finances and relationships. You were able to see how important it was for me to have my friend Mark when confronted with a new career opportunity, as well as see the importance of having a conversation with a close friend that has been in a committed relationship. It is up to you as to whom you elect to spend time with, granting those individuals the golden key to unlock your potential for success with finances and your relationships. If you are looking to get yourself from single to in a relationship, allow yourself to be influenced by the friends that are in long-term successful relationships.

Action: In step 3, write down on either the front or back of the page, depending on how much room you have, the positive financial and relational qualities each friend possesses.

- Write the names of your five closest friends in order on the back of the sheet of paper.

- Next to each name write how you would want that friend to influence you in both areas. For example, you might say, "Susan. Relationship advice because she is in a loving 15 year marriage, and hardly ever argues with her husband".

- Now, for the example that I used, come up with a good question you might ask Susan that will allow you to become more successful in the development of that skill in your own life. So, you might say, "When you are prepared to argue with your spouse, how do you first consult your emotions so you don't explode on your husband?"

CHAPTER 4

Step 4:
Feedback and its Role in Your
Attitudinal Overhaul

Nice job! You made it to step 4. At this point, you have a baseline understanding of what you define as Attitude. You understand who the "Fearful Five" are and the dramatic impact they can play in your life if left un-confronted. In the last chapter you were able to pinpoint some of the favorable and unfavorable characteristics of your five closest friends.

In this chapter you will use the baseline of what you learned about your attitude and the people that are closest to you as a benchmark when viewing your own attitude. If you are still in some type of denial at this point in the book, that you are somehow "different" and not like your friends, I'm here for you. If you truly are not someone who defines yourself with the values of your friends, then it is really yourself that is holding you back from taking life to the next level.

Feedback is the Key to Opening the Next Door of Success

The only way that you are going to be able to do this effectively is by asking for feedback. Never take the assumption of your own analysis. Take the time and consideration of those closest to you. This is done the most effectively through the form of good, honest feedback. I understand that word might sound scary, however, in this chapter I will share with you why it is so vital to your overall attitudinal success in life.

In order for the person providing feedback to know you care, show them. Turn off your cell phone so you are able to focus 100 percent of your attention to the conversation, because the feedback is very important to you. When the individual providing the feedback begins to share their experience working with you, start to take some notes. At this time, if anything is unclear, politely ask them to rephrase it for clarity.

The way to find out how others feel about your current attitude is to ASK for the feedback. In order to effectively do this, you need to be sharing the truth with the one you ask; share with him or her that you are prepared to hear anything. Promise this individual that there will be no repercussion for their honest feedback.

We all need people who will give
us feedback. That's how we improve.

- Bill Gates

Ask for specific examples of times where you displayed a favorable attitude and a time where you displayed a less than ideal attitude. When they share these specific situations, find out how they felt personally. Ask them, if you had responded in a different manner, do they believe the result of the situation may have turned out differently. Regardless of the response, be respectful. It is human nature to become defensive.

"Thank you for your feedback. I want to make sure I'm hearing you correctly. So you believe if I wouldn't have been so stuck in my ways at the board meeting, we might have come up with a more profitable company decision by hearing all other ideas to solve our budget crisis?"

Once you have received and clarified the feedback, be extremely gracious to the one providing the feedback. Have them leave the conversation knowing that, no matter what, this information will be used to help develop a stronger business relationship with your cohorts. I say this because this step becomes really challenging for those that have worked with the same co-workers for 10, 15, or even 20 years.

When the feedback portion is completed, you need to select some form of follow up. Select either a stop-by thank you, follow up e-mail, or a hand written letter to the individual who shared the feedback. Be open, and let them know what action you will take to adjust your attitude. Share with them that because of their courage, it has allowed you to recognize faults and allowed you to learn from those important situations.

After 20 years of being a co-worker, they will know all of your strengths, weaknesses, and skill deficiencies. He or she also feels uncomfortable talking about your weaknesses because they may believe you will think less of them later, maybe at the bar having a conversation about your personal lives. Are you really being a great "friend" if you aren't sharing good honest feedback with someone who asks you for it?

Feedback is Responsible for the Strength & Longevity of the Friendships You Have

Let's take a look at a situation where Negative Attitude might promote fear within to tell the truth, due to the duration of time and friendship you have built with an individual. Never let fear of damaging a relationship scare you away from telling the honest truth. Any good friend will understand, and at the end of the day, truly appreciate the courage you had to share the truth with them.

Imagine for a minute one of your top five friends - let's call him Terry this time - was at the bar with you after work one evening and asked you for feedback. He happens to work with you in the same unit. For years you have noticed that Barry (your boss) becomes rattled every time Terry interrupts him during production meetings, each Tuesday morning at 9:00 am.

You and Terry at the Bar:

Terry: "Hey, I wanted to ask you for some feedback, because I think you're about the only person I feel like I can trust in our department: Do you think I offend Barry at all with some of the jokes I say during our production meetings?"

You: "Terry, I wouldn't think much of it. You know, Berry has three little children at home and doesn't get much sleep (assumption on your part). Hell, I'd get sensitive to your jokes too if I were him."

Terry: "Yeah, I just really enjoy working with you and wouldn't want anything to happen to my job. If you heard anything, you'd tell me if I ever crossed the line with anyone, right?

You: "Of course, Terry, we meet at this bar every Tuesday night, and I have told you the truth the last 5 years we've worked together!"

Terry: "Well, I appreciate that. It is really hard for me to change, and I enjoy the laughs I get from the rest of our department when I tease Barry!"

The following day at work:

The following morning, you notice Terry is cracking jokes about one of the new members that joined the new staff, Gerry. Over in the far cubicle Gerry sits, 5'9", 340 pounds, no hair, and with a large mole on the right side of his forehead. You wonder, "Gosh, I see Terry every Tuesday after work and he has nothing but good things to say about me and my family. I'm curious why he acts that way toward Barry and the staff at work. I think he is getting too close to the line with a few of his jokes. I'm sure Barry will have that conversation with him if things ever get too out of hand."

Next week at the Tuesday morning production meeting:

Alright. Here we are again, the Tuesday production meeting. It's 8:55 am, each person from our staff takes a seat, Terry to my left and Barry to my right. At 9:00 am the meeting begins. Barry starts off the meeting by reviewing the team's to-do list. Like a broken record, Terry rudely interrupts, and cracks a joke about Barry during project updates.

Sitting in the same room, your self-talk probably says, "Well, here we go again, Terry spouting off at the mouth. Classic Terry. One of these days he is really going to get himself into a mess with Barry." In your mind, you might shake it off just like every week and think, "Well, that's just the way he is at work".

Tuesday evening at the bar:

Terry tells you, "Hey, Barry pulled me aside after the meeting this morning. He asked that I please stop interrupting him during project analysis. You don't think he takes what I say serious, do you?"

Like a good friend you think you're being, you click your glass with Terry and say, "Of course not. You know how Barry can be. I'd say pretty sensitive most of the time. Drink up!"

The following week's Production Meeting:

It is the following Tuesday at the production meeting and Terry hasn't changed the attitude he has toward Barry. Butterflies rush through your stomach, recognizing that you should really tell Terry he is making the staff feel really uncomfortable with the comments he is saying to Barry. You think to yourself, "I still want him to be my friend. What if I hurt his feelings? Ah, it'll blow over."

Later that evening at 5:55 pm:

You pull up to the front of the bar, and walk to the right corner where you and Terry have sat together for years, right behind the blue flashing dartboard. You call the bartender over and ask for two lite beers.

As the next five minutes pass, waiting for 6:00 pm, when Terry usually arrives, you think to yourself that tonight you will finally share with him that your co-workers feel uncomfortable with his jokes and behavior at work.

6:00PM:

Gosh, it's always exciting to share a cold one at the end of the day with Terry!

6:05PM:

Well, it's typical that Terry is usually a little bit late. He is probably still futzing around with that car he has been working on in his garage.

6:10PM:

Terry still hasn't arrived.

You: "Okay, now I'm getting a little bit concerned. I'll shoot him a text.

You: "Terry where are you, I have a beer here that's getting warm"

6:15PM:

No Reply

6:20PM:

No Reply

You: "Terry?"

6:35PM

Your phone buzzes. You see a text from Terry.

Terry: "Hey, I have to tell you that I'm a bit disappointed today. Barry pulled me into an office on the way out and told me I was being let go."

You: "What? Terry, how could that be? Did he tell you why?"

Terry: "Yes. Do you remember when I asked you a couple weeks ago to let me know if you heard anything? It was regarding that same conversation. Barry apparently became fed up with the jokes and decided to let me go."

You: "Do you think you will still be able to make it over here so we can talk about it?"

Terry: "I'm sorry. I really have a lot of thinking to do, and I'm going to pass."

Does this situation sound like something you could end up finding yourself in? Due to the fact that you were fearful of sharing honest and candid feedback with your friend, he is now fired. Terry was fired due to an accumulation of poor actions during the production meetings. Terry couldn't help himself, but felt that you could be counted on to have his back; that's why he reached out to you in the first place.

- If this were to happen to you, would you feel like a good friend?

- Would your friendship ever recover?

Have the intestinal fortitude to share with your close friends your observations and concerns as you see them. Trust me, you'll never feel at a lower place than I did in this very moment of my life. When you feel something in your heart that you know is wrong, speak up. At the very minimum, it will allow you to have a conversation about the behaviors you are seeing from one of your closest friends. Because I was a coward and cared more for his feelings than telling him the truth, he lost his job. Now, he has a family of three children with a father that is no longer receiving a paycheck to support them.

In these situations, if you don't have the courage to tell someone something because you feel like it will hurt their feelings, bring it up in a way that shows you care about them and their family.

An approach I could have picked during that first conversation when he asked was, "Terry, I say this because I care about you and your family. I really think it might be in your best interest at work to turn back the dial a bit on the jokes."

Remember, opinions are cheap. This is why everyone has one and is always willing to give theirs out for free. It is easy to turn your head away from the facts of the situation because it allows for easier conversation. Many times, it is harder to share facts. Friends place unconditional trust in you to have their back. Especially in this situation, don't waste an opportunity to tell the truth.

> General reader feedback is usually pretty worthless. 99% of people give feedback that is irrelevant, stupid, or just flat out wrong. But that 1% of people who give good feedback are invaluable.
>
> **-Tucker Max**

Now, because I didn't have the courage to share the truth, I have lost one of my closest friends for the rest of my life.

Both scenarios are important to understand, being the one asking for feedback, and the one of a close friend reaching out to you for feedback. Sharing a positive attitude and telling the truth is, at times, very difficult. It is difficult for you to ask a co-worker or a spouse for the feedback because they might feel uncomfortable providing it. Similar in difficulty is providing feedback to someone else that might indirectly or directly ask for it. You must be the one with the courage to share the truth.

Truth is fact. I would rather have a person that hated me share honest feedback than have a friend I've been with for years observe unfavorable behaviors of me and never say anything.

True friends muster up the courage. They say things like, **"I tell you this because I care"**.

When someone shares this with you, you realize it may have taken him or her days, weeks, or even months to get to the point where they are comfortable enough to share this life changing information with you.

Internally, people dislike hurting each other's feelings. We learned in the second step of this book that the "Fearful Five" love that moment of weakness. For example, the "Negative Nancy" will feed off of that self-doubt, potentially never allowing you to win the battle of the mind to share honest feedback.

This is why in the first portion of the chapter, it is so important, when finding out how others perceive your attitude, that you make a promise to them. Promise that no matter what type of feedback they have for you, it won't affect your relationship with that person (Negative Attitude hates to hear this). Equally as difficult in the second portion, is being the one to offer feedback when you notice something isn't right. I'm sure you would agree with me that the strongest friendships you have are with people that you are comfortable sharing anything with.

We are getting close to overhauling your attitudinal paradigm! In this chapter, you learned the importance of challenging your current perceptions of reality through the form of feedback. In addition, you learned a great deal of the emotion you will be confronted with if you never find the courage to share the truth with someone you love and care about.

Action: In step 4, the challenge is to take a close look at the friends you listed from the action step in Chapter 2 (being your five closest friends).

- Begin by selecting a friend from your list that you would choose if you had to find good honest feedback about how they observe your attitude. Pick a friend that you are able to place your trust in. This is the person that you feel "has your back" in both life and work.

- Set a date when you will muster the courage to fact check the assumptions you are currently making.

- In this step, identify out of your closest friends who you believe is the person that you can place your trust.

  ✓ For example, you might say, "Jeff would be the one I would assume, at this point, to have my back. I have made the commitment to my future success to candidly ask Jeff for his feedback regarding my attitude as he sees it. This will allow me to filter out all of the current assumptions I make regarding the way I see my own attitude."

Next, identify a friend that you feel could really use some feedback. This friend most likely believes you have their back. Come up with a specific time you are going to confront the issue, and why you are willing to share that particular information. Please remember, this exercise is fantastic to build up the courage characteristic warrior on the side of Positive Attitude. This will make uncomfortable conversations you have in your future come far easier because the negative attitude will become weaker in those similar situations moving forward.

  ✓ For example, you might say, "Rick would be the one I feel could use some honest feedback. Every time we get together with a large group of friends, he'll always take the time to pull me aside and share with me the desire he has to get into a relationship. I am going to mention to him some simple observations and recommendations I have seen work in the past for myself and others with similar desires."

Here are some examples of how to deliver your message to your two selected friends:

- Jeff – Gathering Feedback

  - ✓ "Jeff, I promise not to make a big deal out of this, but I was curious if you wouldn't mind sharing with me some feedback of how you observe the way I treat mutual friends?"

- Rick – Giving Feedback

  - ✓ "Rick, I am sharing this with you because I care. I believe if you were to start doing x, y, and z, it might allow you to get into a relationship much faster than the current pace that you are at now."

CHAPTER 5

Step 5:
Who Can Help You Create Your Attitudinal "Why"?

We spent a lot of time in chapter 4 detailing the importance of feedback and what it means related to challenging your current attitudinal perspective. My hope is that, at this point, you haven't over thought it or despised any of your friends after doing so many reflective exercises with them.

In Step 5, we are going to take a look at tangible results. These results come from the way you see the world and how you perceive your friends; this is really where your reality exists. Attitude is formulated from your thoughts and how you view others and situations that arise in your life. Now, using the numbers from the exercise after step 2, let's take a look at which one of your friends (in your opinion) is winning the war on attitude.

- Which one of your friends do you believe has the best attitude?

- Does the person you identified as having the best attitude score with the least amount of points? Remember, the scoring is like golf. Those who score the least, in your opinion, are winning the most!

- If it is different, take a minute to question why that might be.

- Challenge your current perspective and ask, "Which types of tools are they using to win the war on attitude?"

When examining the person you selected as having the best attitude will be based on your idea of reality. Truth becomes reality of what you believe as being true or correct.

For example, when you were young, your parents might have told you that one of your greatest assets in life will be the home you live in; this couldn't be further from the truth. Your attitude and reality were based on the perspective of your parents. If never challenged, it is likely you still carry those same beliefs.

I'd be willing to bet that the person you selected as having the best attitude currently has the results you desire. If your goal is to become a millionaire, you might assess your friend Bill as winning the war on attitude against the "Media Monger". His personal finance and relational results don't seem to change based on who is winning and losing in this year's election cycle for the presidency. I'll bet if you summed up the courage to ask Bill about this situation, he'd tell you that this year is going to be a lot like last year in terms of his personal income. Consistent growth is a result of the choices you make based on the situation you are given on a daily and yearly basis.

Now, using the person you selected as having the best attitude (scoring the least amount of points), let's assess what they scored on your attitude worksheet.

If the person you selected has a zero, I would suggest you stop what you're doing, pick up the phone, talk with him or her, and find out their formula to success. Start walking the way they do, eat the way they do, drive the way they do, make dinner the way they do, etc. Well, you get my point. The truth is, no matter if the friend you selected scored a low number or a high number, it is all based on your reality; how you view the world.

The template for assessment will not always be totally accurate for every individual using it.

For example, let's say while analyzing yourself, you emphasized the four words that I used in my own assessment: Persistence, Happiness, Loving, and Helping. These particular warriors battling on the Positive Attitude side hold a high level of significance on the way I, in particular, view the battleground.

If you feel strongly that forgiving is the most important, essentially being a franchise player on your team, it is likely that you feel that "Pessimistic Peter" is one of the strongest opponents to defeat on the battlegrounds in your everyday life. However, if you feel that "Worry Wart" is the most powerful opponent against you, it is likely that you place a large value on the development of the warrior on the Positive Attitude side, known as optimism.

I encourage each of my friends that complete this step to really think about the qualities in a Positive Attitude warrior they are looking for; each mental battleground is a bit different individual to individual. Maybe, as you look at the results, the numbers validate the story you thought was truth all along.

Anne came in dead last (scoring the most points). She always seems to **put herself first**, has been **in and out of 4 marriages**, is $50,000 in **personal debt**, and can **never seem to find the time** to spend with her three and four year old.

Let's use this situation. If this is the truth as you see it, I'm willing to assume you value the following: Leadership, Relational Trust, Financial Strength, and Time spent with loved ones. Now, take those qualities and add them to your Positive Attitude side, as they will play an important role toward the completion of this book.

Identifying those that surround you as having or lacking a positive attitude can be a challenging exercise. Internally, your self-talk may cause you to debate with yourself saying your friend "isn't always like that". This is why, while evaluating your friends, it is very important to use your "gut" when answering yes or no, allocating points to each of the "Fearful Five" warriors your friends face on a day-to-day basis. Your gut will give you the instant summary or accumulation of actions in each category.

See the use of your "gut" as you would hitting the equals sign on a calculator.

It allows you to come up with an instant analysis of each situation, challenging it against your own attitudinal paradigm.

At this point, you might be thinking the following:

- "I don't have the time to be helpful."

- "I'd be more encouraging, but Betty always messes up the project at work."

- "I understand loving my family is important, but I have to work 14 hour days just to stay ahead."

Don't worry. You're not alone. Many people are fighting these battles daily. To acquire the positive attitudinal qualities you desire in your closest friend will not come free or easy. They come at a cost, a significant one at that. It is known as energy. We all have it. Your friend that you identified with makes the choice to push their choice in words and actions toward their vision, regardless of what they are feeling at that time. Their choices are a reflection of themself. They have integrity and want to protect the way others view them; their reputation is important.

Reputation is a reflection of the accumulation of choices that you have made up until this point in your life.

Those that have a strong vision, a strong "attitudinal why", protect this, regardless of their energy level, on a daily basis. I'm sure while you are reading this, you could probably think of that one friend on your list that protects this better than others. This person, no matter what the circumstance, will always have his or her "attitudinal why" at the front of their mind. Let me create a quick scenario of how your friend protects his or her reputation.

In this situation, the friend you identified as having a positive attitude is called Bob. Evaluating your friend, you recognize him as one that possesses the qualities and results you desire. He has $1,000,000 in the bank, a loving wife of 25 years, and two beautiful children. As a local financial advisor, Bob is known in the community as someone with a great amount of integrity.

Early on a winter day, Bob has someone pull the door handle open to his office downtown. As the door rings, Bob is met by a tall man who has covered his face with a ski mask. The person that arrived has known Bob for years; however, with the ski mask on, Bob has no way of knowing.

The intruder yells out, "Bob, I know you have millions. Give me all of it, or I'll shoot you." Realizing this is a life or death situation, Bob runs back to the vault and unlocks the door to his $1,000,000 in cash he keeps on hand at the store.

Bob screams, "Please, take the money, just don't hurt my family!" As the robber peels out of the parking lot with the cash, Bob runs to call 911. As 911 replies to the call, officers arrive minutes later.

The law informant officer that first arrives asks, "Did you activate the alarm system?"

Bob replies softly, "No. He walked in like my many other customers."

The officer replies, "That's a shame. If you would have notified us earlier, we may have been able to catch him."

The officer and Bob continue to discuss what needs to be done moving forward from this dreadful circumstance. During the conversation outside, the officer notices something on the pavement near a set of tracks. In the distance, close to the front of the shop, is a wallet. As the officer grabs the wallet, he checks the identification and asks Bob if the man looks familiar. It was the wallet of an old junior broker Bob employed and worked with many years ago.

The officer asks, "Bob, do you know this man?"

In disbelief, shaking his head, Bob replies, "That's him. That's the guy who took the money."

The officer replies on his radio, "Calling out to all officers nearby to look for plates 867-SFY."

Minutes later, the officer gets a reply back, "We found the vehicle sir." Turned upside down in an abandoned cornfield laid the Green 1998 Ford Taurus the robber used as the escape vehicle. Bob instantly asks the police officer for coordinates to go and see his former junior broker named Tyler. As the officer and Bob arrive, in the distance lies the body of Tyler. Upon arrival, Tyler was clinging for his own life.

Bob approaches the vehicle stating, "We need help. Call an ambulance!"

Bob asks Tyler, "Are you okay?"

Tyler replies, "Bob, I am so sorry. I never meant to take your money. Times have been rough and I couldn't think of any other way to make it."

Bob replies, "Let's make sure we get you taken care of first kid."

A month later, the first responding officer and Bob show up to the hospital where Tyler was receiving care for his injuries after the accident.

Bob leans in to Tyler and says, "Get well soon kid."

The officer pays his respects to Tyler and walks out of the room with Bob.

Together as they turn the first corner the officer says, "Boy, we are going to be able to put him away for years for what he did to you."

Bob responds, "Officer, there will be no punishment. I am not going to press charges. This was a young kid that made a grave error in judgment that is paying for his actions more than enough at this time."

If this were a novel I would finish the narrative, but as you can see, this situation was built to prove a point. Bob has very strong values and a clearly defined "attitudinal why". He values the importance of personal growth; building a professional empire allowing him to store $1,000,000 in cash on hand at the store. He values helpfulness; at a time in the story where most would want to resort to violence for what Tyler had done to Bob, Bob sought medical attention first. Lastly, you could probably gather that Bob has spent many hours in the development of his strongest warrior, the ability to forgive.

Don't waste years of your life holding grudges for what others have done to you. Whether they stole your time, money (like Bob), resources, influence, or power; **move on**. This is the only action that you can perform that shows you are winning that battle against the Negative Attitude. If you allow grudges to stay in your brain, you might as well start charging them rent, because otherwise they aren't doing you much good. Make the sacrifice, be the bigger person, and **move on**.

If you are reviewing this situation and you think of a situation where you do not believe that you will be able at this time to offer forgiveness, that is okay. You have made the **CHOICE** to pick up this book and overhaul your attitudinal strengths and weaknesses. The good news for you is that attitude is developed over time and can always be changed. It isn't going to be easy to win the war versus the Negative Attitude. Negative Attitude doesn't care about how much sleep you had the night before or how many times you were beaten down by others the day when you really need to forgive. It is up to you to have the responsibility to own those emotions that might lead to negative behavior.

I will assure you, the closest friend you have that has a positive attitude and you feel develops the best relationships, would tell you it **isn't easy**. Likely, they are dealing with the same challenges that you deal with on a daily basis. I understand everyone's situation is specific to his or her own situation, however, it is important to have the respect to still push forward and realize it is the negative attitude that is infiltrating your thoughts with doubt.

The Negative Attitude grows strong very quickly, each time you make the choice to watch the daily news, surf Facebook for 5 hours, or get lost in others' lives vicariously through Snapchat. It plants its roots deeper and deeper, pushing you to your limit, defeating those that don't have a clearly defined "attitudinal why" each and every day. For most, they don't even realize it is happening. Negative Attitude requires far less time and effort to grow big and strong.

It really is an unfair game, but you need to recognize that to remain vigilant in your fight. Negative Attitude is the guy at the gym who works out once a month and has six-pack abs. Positive Attitude development growth is long, boring, and much harder to develop. With that being said, the outcome and level of gratitude you'll feel when you succeed, winning with the Positive Attitude, will be like nothing you've experienced before. Keep working, fight hard every day, don't forget your vision and your "attitudinal why", and you will find success.

In order to best prepare for the real world, let's use a simple example of a thought that might pop into your head at the end of a long day at work:

"Well, I'd probably be cheery too if I didn't come home to any children and only worked 30 hours a week!"

Number one, please don't use blame as an excuse to not display the attitude you wish to have. In this phrase, it is simply a physical emotion that is beating this person's "attitudinal why" to change and display the attitude he or she wants others to view. You must have the gumption and ability to recognize this to be able to make the change to face this emotion. When a warrior from your negative attitude side pops up, recognize that it is there, and make the choice to beat it. A person that clearly has a well-defined "attitudinal why" in this situation might think the following:

"Well, I see that Tiffany was quite chipper today. Although I am tired, I will make the choice to compliment her and allow her positive energy to become contagious!"

Awesome! This is very well done. Recognize the attitude you desire. Identify your physical state or the Negative Attitude that might be holding you back from displaying those emotions. Finally, look for the best win-win scenario. Give a compliment to those that are displaying the behaviors you desire, even when you're not. In time, they will become contagious to you because you're willing to accept them! Nice Job!

In this step, you learned the importance of having and protecting your "attitudinal why." If you don't have that clearly defined, Negative Attitude will recognize this and take advantage. Negative Attitude will create an "attitudinal why" for you if you aren't careful! Don't get stuck or caught up in what others are doing or the behaviors they are displaying. Continue to work hard at your "attitudinal why" and success will find you. If you end up losing a few friends that nurtured Negative Attitude, then it may be the perfect time to weed the garden and grow!

Action: In step 5, circle the friend on your sheet of paper you selected as having the most positive attitude, and clearly defined "attitudinal why". Did that person receive the lowest score in your analysis from the previous chapters?

- On the back of your paper, write down the name of the person you identify as having the most "positive attitude".

- Next to that person, write down why you feel this particular person has a positive attitude. Explain some of the individual battles you feel he or she is winning against some of the warriors (Raging Recruiter, Worry Wart, etc.). How are they able to perform some of those actions? What are the results they are receiving in their personal life? Are they one that is able to develop strong relationships? Based on what you know about your friend, would you consider him or her one that is able to gain influence at work?

- Underneath the person you select, draw a circle. In that circle write the words, "My Attitudinal Why". Take the positive behavior this person displays with gratitude, and think what you would like to place into your own "Attitudinal Why".

For Example –

"My Attitudinal Why" – Caring, Loving, Faith, Hope, Friendship, Success, Wife, Relationship, Money, Etc.

- This should only take a moment. Take your cell phone, and set a timer for 5 minutes; this will allow you to stay focused and propel you to step 6.

Example –

- Rick – He is definitely winning the battle against the "Raging Recruiter".

  ✓ I work with my friend Rick. Every day at work, I see him being pulled into a water cooler conversation he doesn't want to be a part of, yet he remains positive. Rick isn't one to take advantage of an environment where the Negative Attitude can grow. I can learn from this behavior: the next

time I'm in a water cooler, slander filled
conversation, I will remain positive.

- **"My Attitudinal Why"**

  ✓ I want to be defined by behaviors my friend Rick
  displays on a daily basis. I want to have the courage
  and conviction to stay true to my "why" no matter
  what. I want to be defined as one that loves, cares,
  shares, gives, is a loving husband, and can provide
  plenty of money to my family. I will stay true to
  this vision and only exhibit behaviors that would
  be evidence of this.

CHAPTER 6

Step 6:
How Will I Implement my,
"Attitudinal Why"?

In step 5, you spent some more time identifying the positive behaviors you desire. Mirroring and matching some of those behaviors will be the fertilizer you can use to create an environment for your Positive Attitude and "Attitudinal Why" to grow!

In step 6, we will spend time discussing how you will be implementing your attitude overhaul mission. I will share with you some of the key factors for success in the battle between Positive and Negative Attitude. I will be giving you some perspective on how your behavior choices will make a significant impact on how you would like others to perceive you, as you defined in your "Attitudinal Why" at the end of the last chapter.

At this point in the book, you have spent some time identifying who you believe has the most positive attitude amongst those you choose to spend time with. I'm going to share with you one of the key tools a person with Positive Attitude will keep in their arsenal and deploy on their weakest day.

The friend you have with the best Positive Attitude, through your eyes, is likely to have developed this warrior for years; they weren't trained overnight. This warrior was developed to give your Positive Attitude team a member that is phenomenal at fighting off Negative Attitude because of focus. The primary power of this warrior is known as discipline.

Confidence comes from discipline and training.

-Robert Kiyosaki

Each person reading this book runs into unfair situations. You might be reading this chapter while being in the worst debt financially of your life. You might be concerned about taking a job at a new company because it will affect the security you have now. You're not alone. That is why, in this chapter, I will help you discover what you'll need to do to have the Positive Attitude warriors work for you, and it won't feel like work at all.

A person that consistently shares a Positive Attitude with the world has built a reputation over the course of time, displaying behaviors we can expect from them. As you probably can guess by now, it is going to take work. It will require you to step outside your comfort zone and make choices that aren't easy. Literally, get to the point where you confront Negative Attitude on the battleground and say, "There is no way you will beat me to today". This is where your life will turn for the best!

Implementing positive behaviors into your daily life will increase confidence amongst your Positive Attitude team within. It will share with your Positive Attitude warriors that you are there for them through the hard days and the easy days. When the day comes that you choose to turn your life around (I hope that is today) you will feel an immediate impact within. Passion will begin to seep through your veins, because today is the day you broke the chains of the shackles of your limiting beliefs.

Many of my friends will tell me I believe I have a Positive Attitude, but I'm not getting the results I desire.

- Do my actions really become a reflection of my friends? The simple answer is yes.

Let's use a simple baking example to put this into perspective.

In our own minds, we each tend to believe the choices we are making are the best, based on the situation at hand. Thus, look at your brain as a large bowl of thought (this where your self-talk is battling over your attitudinal energy). In this bowl, you have your own Positive and Negative Attitude squaring off with one another consistently throughout the day. Some would argue this alone is hard enough to handle! Then, add to that bowl all of the thoughts and dispositions your friends share with you; it becomes a part of the mix.

Essentially, the larger the number of friends you identified as losing the war against the "Fearful Five" is seen as the strongest spice in your bowl. He or she has the ability to completely ruin everything! Have the courage to look at your thoughts candidly. If you decide to "figure out" a way to make the dish work with such a strong spice, then go right ahead. But at some point, if you have a friend or friends with a set of overwhelming Negative Attitudes, I would suggest it might be time to dump the bowl out and start from scratch.

When you do this, it will give you a breath of fresh air, opening the freedom of choice you have been searching for. Now I'm giving you the opportunity to say that it's okay to let those friends go. Start living your life exhibiting the behaviors of the Positive Attitude. Build the reputation and power necessary to develop the life of your dreams!

In the NFL, each team wishes they had the dream quarterback, such as Aaron Rodgers of the Green Bay Packers. He is a dynamic player who has the arm strength of Hercules, the legs of a gazelle, and wit of a Harvard law student. I'm here today to share with you that this is the type of Positive Attitude warrior you will need in order to win the war on Attitude. However, just because we all want an Aaron Rodgers on our team, doesn't mean we can magically take him from one team and add him to our own. He developed his skills over time, sitting and watching behind the hall of fame quarterback Brett Favre.

In a few moments, I'm going to share with you that we each have an Aaron Rodgers on our own team. He just isn't developed yet. It is going to take tremendous time, effort, sacrifice, accountability, and responsibility to develop him. Right now your Aaron Rodgers is watching you. It's time to start sharing with him the right way to do things around here (in your brain). This dynamic Positive Attitude warrior currently sitting on your bench is known as discipline.

Discipline strengthens the mind so that it becomes impervious to the corroding influence of fear.

-Bernard Law Montgomery

Discipline is a tool that will unlock so many doors for you in your life. If you spend time developing this warrior within, it will pay you back physically, emotionally, and financially.

The trainer's manual to build this warrior starts with these three steps:

Willingness

First is **willingness**: Commit to these changes and begin to develop excitement for the results that are coming your way. The willingness muscle of discipline is only developed when supported by your internal "Attitudinal Why". You need to have strong conviction of the new behaviors you are working to develop. If your "Attitudinal Why" isn't strong enough, Negative Attitude will recognize and immediately take advantage. It'll loiter in your gut and mind. This one, I promise, will be the hardest to shake.

Willingness needs to be the strongest muscle discipline needs to develop. If you have an underdeveloped willingness, you'll never hear the voice of your Positive Attitude sharing the reasons why you're pushing through the hard times to create change. Developing willingness will create persistence during hard times. This is the first and most critical muscle to develop of discipline to get started on the track of Positive Attitude behaviors.

Awareness

Second, teach discipline the quality of **awareness**; share with discipline what you want and what you are willing to do in order to receive the benefit of the positive behaviors you set out to display. Have you heard the term "gut-check" time? This asks individuals to perform an action based solely on their feelings and pre-dispositions. It compels you to indicate if the decisions you are making in regards to relationships, social life, and finances are where your vision and goals align. If you don't have your " Attitudinal Why" defined based on where you would like to be some day, discipline will run out of breath. It will die due to a lack of oxygen from your Positive Attitude.

Awareness is a muscle of discipline that can become stronger with the use of consistent Positive Attitude behaviors, creating a benefit to you known as momentum. Momentum is used by the Positive Attitude to assist in your development of behaviors that align closer to your goals. See momentum as the lungs of discipline. This is why it is so important to write your goals (these can be the behaviors you listed in step 5 as your "Attitudinal Why") daily, assuring your mind of where you are soaring. If you have a lack of awareness and lose sight of your goals, momentum will surely run out of oxygen. Negative Attitude will always notice when this happens, recognizing this as an excellent opportunity to fill your mind with doubt. Next time it is "gut-check" time for you, you'll have built up the aerobic capacity of momentum that keeps your discipline alive for years! Before you know it, on the days you wake up with little sleep, didn't get the chance to finish the project at work, and the baby is crying, you will still "make time" to complete the tasks that get you closer to achieving your vision!

Awareness of the Negative Attitude penetrating your thought zone is one of the most important keys to victory of the mind. Consistently following the patterns of what it will take to achieve your goals is what will also add more oxygen for discipline to function. These are known as the "feel good" emotions. Feeling empowered, confident, and explosive is what you'll need to keep Positive Attitude alive.

Commitment to Habit

Third is **commitment to habit**. It is widely known that it takes 21 days to turn a consistent action from a few days into something that doesn't feel like work any longer. Turbo-charging your discipline to the mind-set of waking up an hour early every day to work on a skill you have been trying to develop for years is worth it! This is fueled by the goals you developed for yourself. Commitment works well with consistent progress. Build this muscle by asking your closest friend, or friends, to hold you accountable to your new desired behaviors. Have the confidence to share with your friends that you are committed to changing and need their help. More likely than not, your friend would be happy to do it, and along the journey you will notice that might become one of your most trusted friendships. Trust is developed by asking others for their help.

Your friends are there for your support. They will keep you focused on your vision, strengthening the commitment muscle every time your friend positively reinforces a good behavior they see you perform. Please, please, please don't fear sharing your attitudinal goals with your friends; the good ones will help and support your Positive Attitude growth!

When commitment becomes strong, discipline will find it much easier to make tough decisions.

For example, commitment is the muscle discipline will flex when you are driving home from work, haven't had lunch, and really need something to eat. While developing your "Attitudinal Whys" to change, you told yourself you would quit making poor eating choices. Since your "Attitudinal Why" is strong, and you have committed yourself to change, you choose not to stop and pick up fast food. You make a wiser decision by going home and eating some almonds to hold you over until you are prepared to make a healthy dinner for yourself that evening.

Sharing the qualities of discipline is important to understanding why you might feel some of your friends have a Positive Attitude. In the beginning of the chapter, we discussed who you thought might have a Positive Attitude, and then assessed the scores they received from previous chapters to shed some light on where they are winning on the war of the mind. It is my belief and recommendation from this chapter that you need to develop discipline. Using this skill will allow you to align your focus and quit making excuses for your current actions. You can change.

In step 6, we discussed the importance of awareness of self-talk occurring in your mind. We learned that the battle for your energy through self-talk takes place every single day of your life and creates your behaviors and results in life. Finally, you learned how you can turn your "Attitudinal Why" into a reality. It is done through the many different layers and muscles that are required for discipline to work effectively in the growth of your Positive Attitude.

Action: In step 6, the primary focus will be on how you are going to be implementing these new Attitude Behaviors into your life.

- At this point, you might need an additional sheet of paper.

- Think of a time where you were at your absolute weakest on an attitudinal level. For example, if you are often times tired after work, you might decide to stop into a fast food restaurant and eat a double cheeseburger instead of going home to eat a salad.

- Use this situation, or one similar to it, and write down how you are going to deal with the Negative Attitude when it bubbles up the next time. It is vital to have a plan, because if you don't, Negative Attitude will find out and prevent you from accomplishing your goals. Like the old saying goes, "If you fail to plan, plan to fail!"

- This should only take a moment. Take your cell phone and set a timer for 5 minutes. This will allow you to stay focused and propel you to step 7.

- What situations do I put myself in where I am at my weakest against Negative Attitude?

  ✓ *I am a single guy who works twelve-hour days. When I get done, the last thing I want to even think about doing is cooking dinner for myself. Being weak and unfocused at this time, I'll, more likely than not, pull through a drive through, and it usually isn't the healthy choice!*

- Taking the example from above, how will you address this same situation the next time it arises?

  ✓ *The next time that I feel tired and weak, I need to remember my "Attitudinal Why". I need to even say my goals and vision out loud to create a positive momentum for a more disciplined approach. I am strong. Next time, I will make the choice, go home, and eat healthy!*

CHAPTER 7

Step 7: Overhauling Your Pre-Existing Beliefs

You are doing a great job! I'm so excited for you and the progress you've made so far during this book. I'm confident that you have really felt and thought deeply about some of the choices you've made up until this point in your life.

In this step, we will take a close look at the importance of eliminating the ego, speaking directly to the self-talk that says, "Well, I have a degree. I deserve that company position." In order to evolve and display the behaviors that you desire, it will be truly up to you and your level of commitment to turn your life around.

Let's first start off by speaking to the pre-existing belief on education. There is nothing more frustrating than seeing someone with less education than you making more money than you. Of course, we have all heard the stories of the ultra-successful going from rags to riches. However, that is only a very tiny majority of the population. In America, the unemployment rate of those with Bachelor's degrees is much smaller than those that possess no education at all. Regardless of your education level, push your ego out of the way in these situations, and work up the courage to ask your friends questions. Be absolutely shameless. If they are getting better results than you, accept it and move forward.

Earning money is far different from earning a degree in college. Yes, again, I hear your frustration. If you're reading this book and received a prestigious degree from Harvard in quantum physics, money doesn't care. This is probably something your friend that is receiving positive financial results has figured out! The market is going to pay you based on your value to the marketplace. Having a degree in quantum physics could be a valuable asset to NASA. However, there are only a few locations that NASA would hire for that particular skill.

The marketplace pays skilled labor. Some of the wealthiest people you may or may not know are the plumbers, electricians, roofers, and contractors. Negative Attitude will promote ego to drive you from accepting this reality. Ego will tell you that since you know quantum physics, you need to find that exact job. Ego will tell you that since you are skilled, you deserve a job. Crush the EGO. The most effective way to combat this is by looking at your skills from a different perspective than what your college professor told you.

Put your skills to work and look for job openings that require the skills you have, rather than a specific job title. You will find lucrative positions available that are looking for the skills you have. So, don't become envious of your friend making more money than you. Take responsibility, share gratitude toward their success, and remember it is their financial success you desire. If you continue to feel sorry for yourself, money still won't care. Put yourself in the best position to be paid by the marketplace.

What makes this friend different? Why do you believe they are successful?

Without thinking that your friend is lucky, or is living in a situation that is easier to be successful than you, truly think of reasons why they are successful.

Use the following sentence starters below:

- Tom typically has a _____ attitude.

- Tom has these skills: _____,
  _____, and _____.

- Because of these skills, I believe Tom receives
  $_____ a year in income.

- If I were to adopt some of those same qualities in my
  position, I should expect to receive about
  $_____ a year in income.

Challenge your current beliefs. What makes them different from you right at this moment? Based on the answers you gave above, why are some of those qualities important to your personal and financial success?

- If you were to apply those skills and Positive Attitude techniques, how would that impact your life?

- Do you believe you would double your own personal income?

- Do you believe you would begin to gain more influence in your life?

- Do you believe you would obtain a closer relationship with your son or daughter?

- After you assess the qualities of the closest friend you have that possess the strongest Positive Attitude characteristics, ask yourself, "How are they winning the battle?"

- Be shameless; a good friend will be happy to share. People love vulnerability. It shows you're real. You may be surprised how much more trust will blossom in having thorough conversations.

Here is how the conversation might go between you and the friend you selected with the most Positive Attitude characteristics:

Cassi: "Hey Tom. I have to ask you, every time I go out to eat with you and your wife Kim, you always seem to be completely in love and are never distracted. How do you do it?"

Tom: "Cassi, I really appreciate your kind words. I can say, it didn't happen overnight. It took some honest commitments and sacrifices to get to where we are today."

Cassi: "Tom, I would like to ask you some questions, because I value your success both at work and in your relationship with Kim. Do you have a few minutes?"

Tom: "Absolutely. How can I help?"

Cassi: "Recently, I read a book on Attitude Overhaul (hey, that's the book you're reading right now!). In the book, it mentioned a few key items I found out I deal with on a daily basis that I never could quite figure out a solution to. However, out of all the friends I have, I see you as one that handles stress, worry, and distraction the best."

"Where I struggle is when I get home from work, and all I want to do is kick my feet up. It wasn't until I read this book that I realized a lot of the opinions I have formed of the world were based on values shared on the evening news."

"Tom, at work I notice, during lunch, when our cohorts get to talking about politics, you just seem to stay out of it. How are you not influenced?"

Tom: "Boy, Cassi. I didn't know you were this serious about changing your attitude and challenging your current perspectives."

"At work, it is difficult to not share my opinion, because I definitely have one. However, why should it be my role to pollute the minds of my co-workers with the reality of my opinion?"

"Cassi, remember, opinions are cheap, because everyone is willing to share theirs. It is facts that are more valuable, and typically they don't come from conversations about politics."

A key takeaway anyone could have from this conversation is the way that Tom handled himself. Right away, I noticed how Tom didn't judge Cassi for coming up and speaking with him about his attitude. Tom realizes that it probably took a tremendous amount of courage to come up to him and be able to have that conversation. Friends like Tom are the ones you need to surround yourself with. These are people that are open, willing to help, and are living a life which you desire.

Curiosity is a word that I believe is often times not talked about in personal development books. Amongst the many that you have probably read, they share with you the principles to success. They share the 10 keys to getting the life you desire, or the 5 fundamentals to living the life of your dreams.

We keep moving forward, opening new doors, and doing new things, because we're curious and curiosity keeps leading us down new paths.

-Walt Disney

Don't get me wrong; I believe there is great value in each book that you read. Even if you find value in just one sentence, it could potentially change the direction of your life. However, often I'll hear from my personal friends that take the time to read the personal development books, that their life never seems to change for the better. It is my observation that people aren't curious enough to compare what they are reading to their own lives. This is another reason I am so passionate about the information that I am sharing with you in this book: to help individuals spend more time looking at themselves internally to make necessary changes to achieve the results they desire.

I find it astounding that most people live their lives on autopilot. Simply waking up in the morning, drinking a hot cup of coffee, and heading in to work a job they hate. They come home from work upset (because they hate their job) and pass that anger onto their family. These are the individuals that are looking for someone or something to blame their unhappiness on. You can't blame your occupation, bills, children or spouse. Look in the mirror. It's you. You are in control of your life; don't let life control you!

You may feel that you are at "rock-bottom" at this very moment, but I can promise you there is someone out there right now living in a situation ten times worse.

Just remember that.

Remember that the next time you go home to your children and they are acting a little rambunctious, and you are feeling irritable from your long work day not to pass your irritation on to them. It is important to reflect on where that irritability is actually coming from. Your emotions are like a boomerang. What goes around comes back around. For everything to change in your life, you must be the one to change first.

Personally, recognizing this was very challenging to complete, but I decided to take action. Initially, I would develop the excuse of saying, "I don't have enough time to implement these newly desired behaviors into my life". With reflection, I returned my focus to my commitment to my "Attitudinal Why", but second, each day I made sure that I scheduled a 5-10 minute meeting with each day just to breathe. This has allowed me to candidly review my behaviors each day and be honest with myself about which behaviors that I felt aligned or didn't align with my "Attitudinal Why".

Step 7 is vitally important for the longevity of the success that you will have against the continual Negative Attitude you will be presented with in your life. As I mentioned in the beginning portion of this book, I am speaking to the 99% of people out there that lean on their friends for help and advice. Of course, there will always be that 1% that have the fortitude to turn it all around themselves. If that is you, please don't let me be the roadblock that keeps you from overhauling your attitudinal behaviors. However, if you're like me and fall in the 99%, you need to take a look at your friends and ask for help.

Being curious is also helpful in growing and maintaining the friendship with the friend you have found to have attitudinal goals that align the most with your own. Did you know that you are more likely to build trust with a friend that you ask for help? Trust grows faster when you ASK for help! This will omit making assumptions about your friend's perspective, which will help to strengthen your friendship with them.

- Ask, "Why does my friend Jim make twice as much money as me?"

- Ask, "Why does my friend Rick always seem happy in love, and is maintaining a 25 year relationship with his wife?"

The change as I mentioned, however, is to not play the blame game while going through this exercise. It is best to write down on a sheet of paper the skills and behaviors he or she has that you admire.

It is equally important to identify and select one of your five closest friends that you consider as winning in each of these areas of life. If the results they are getting align with your "Attitudinal Why", you need to have the courage to reach out and ask for help.

Finally, continue to keep some aspect of curiosity in your mindest. Trust me, this isn't easy. Naturally, the Negative warriors are going to want to fill your brain with reasons to blame others for your short falls in life. It is up to you to develop your Positive warriors to replace the negativity and blame with visions of success, curiosity and optimism.

During this step, you might find personal resistance from your brain saying, "Well, sure, if I inherited the farm, I'd have a million dollars too." STOP IT.

In step 7, you learned the importance of curiosity can be to challenge your pre-existing attitudinal beliefs. You have the power of choice. If it is required that you go to school for two years to learn the skills he or she has to run a profitable farm, then go for it. Stay curious. What would you have to sacrifice to get there? Ask how or what you could do to help create those results with the resources you have available, starting today.

Action: In step 7, the primary focus is on challenging your pre-existing beliefs that might be holding you back. These beliefs may be scaring your Curiosity warrior off the playing field each day, which is holding you back from a better-desired outcome.

* Grab another sheet of paper if you need to...

* Identify an area in your life or personal characteristic that you believe is holding you back from achieving your full, desired potential. For example, "I have worked at the same company for 20 years without a promotion. I guess I just have to wait until I'm on the 'boss's good side' in order to get promoted".

  ✓ How can you use what you have learned to move forward? Maybe you could schedule some time to meet with your boss and discuss the situation. Be *curious.* Ask about what it would take in order to receive a promotion. Leave no assumption or stone un-turned; if your perspective isn't fact checked, you will lose every time.

- This should only take a moment. Take your cell phone and set a timer for 5 minutes. This will allow you to stay focused and propel you to the final step, step 8!

List a few of your known pre-existing beliefs (be honest).

1. *"I have worked at the same company for 20 years without a promotion. I guess I just have to wait until I'm on the 'boss's good side' in order to get promoted".*

2. *"Sure, if I was like Jeff and worked 30 hours a week, I'd have plenty of energy too to be cheerful at night when I come home from work. I'm confident that is the reason why he is in a long term relationship."*

How will you be challenging each of the beliefs listed above?

1. *I will challenge this belief, starting by scheduling a meeting with my boss. This will allow me to find out the facts of the situation, allowing me to move quickly toward my financial goals.*

2. *During the 5-10 minutes I spend meeting with myself, I will take the time to recognize and validate the results Jeff is getting. Then, I will make a commitment that, moving forward, I won't allow myself to blame Jeff for getting results I desire.*

CHAPTER 8

Step 8:
Proactive Action Necessary
to Install Your New Beliefs

Congratulations! You have made it. We are finally here, the final step you'll need to officially defeat Negative Attitude in your life forever! Are you ready yet?

At this point in the book, I have shared with you exactly what is happening on the battleground of your mind on a daily basis. Essentially, what I have done is handed you the microscope to get an internal view. In this chapter, I am going talk in depth about having awareness and the responsibility for choices and outcomes that have occurred in your life.

You now should have identified common excuses that you may have been using as scapegoats for not achieving your goals in life. You have the awareness. Your Positive Attitude team is prepared and is ready to get to work for you. Moving forward, you will have the awareness of the "Fearful Five", and the attitudinal strength to not let them disrupt your progress at any time.

The final step places an emphasis on responsibility. I will share with you the importance of being truthful with yourself, so that you never create a false sense of reality. The final step places an emphasis on responsibility. I would like to share with you the importance of being truthful to yourself, so that you never create a false sense of reality. Lastly, I will expose one of the valuable warriors of Negative Attitude; although it isn't a part of the "Fearful Five," it is essential to defeat in order to win the Attitudinal warfare; Fear.

Awareness ⤳

Awareness is one of the primary aspects of becoming successful with identifying your own attitude.

For example, you might have a friend of yours that grew up in a negative household, with negative parents who shared a poor lifestyle. Based on your friend's past, they may not have even been aware that there is a better life out there. Have the courage to share what you've learned in this book with them. Offer to help them. You might be surprised by how much benefit you will gain yourself by offering a helping hand to make your closest friends more aware.

Awareness is important, you must make the decision to take action for your own life, based on the information you have read from this book. Awareness without taking responsibility is like trying to run a marathon without eating the proper meal prior. You have to fuel your body to be successful. You have to be the fuel that ignites your own life by taking responsibility.

Something I find interesting is when people don't take responsibility for their own results. I encourage you to develop the awareness for your actions and "own-up" to your actions. Make the commitment from this point forward to take responsibility for every result. Doing so will put you back into the driver seat of your life and the ability to make the changes necessary. You'll be able to assure your mind that you have control over the situation.

For example, if I were to tell you right now you were diagnosed with a serious illness, what would be your first reaction?

Would you shout out and ask, "Why did this happen to me?" With this perspective, you are giving up control of your attitude; losing control and trying to place blame. The best thing you can do is to take responsibility for it. Do not dwell on something that is outside of your control. When you take responsibility for it, you are back in the driver's seat and can allow your mind to find solutions to fix this problem.

Many individuals may have a problem with this example. I get it. Serious illness is a hard topic to talk about because each of us has had someone in our life affected by it. When bad things arrive in your life, or the lives of others, they don't want to take responsibility for a circumstance they feel they didn't have control over. Again, I still encourage you from this point forward to take responsibility. You'll never be able to grow and develop into something that is exceptional if you don't feel like you have control over your own life and all of the results that come from it. Be curious and take the lead in looking up treatment options/remedies to fix the situation. Then, when you have extended all your options, **move on** and live your life and when another problem arises take control!

Now that you are aware and have taken responsibility for your results up until this part of your life, it is time to prepare your mind for future situations that might arise. To live your life consistently with responsibility, you will have to start to act, and not react, to future situations.

For instance, this is why pilots require so many hours of flying before they are able to go out and fly on their own. This extensive training is done to assure the passengers, themselves and everyone else that they will be prepared to handle any situation that is presented to them in the sky.

This is the type of mentality you need to begin to develop in your own life. In order to best prepare your mind for this, it is important that at the end of the day, just before you go to bed, you plan out your next day. Write down what might happen and what struggles you might face. If the project went wrong, how will I react to my co-worker?

The goal in doing this isn't to make you become more paranoid about situations that haven't even occurred yet in your life, but to serve as a place to store your thoughts or fears. Then you are prepared to handle most situations that are presented to you. You'll at that point been prepared, have taken responsibility, and will begin the process of implementing what is needed to fix the issue.

Writing your goals and expectations of each of these will help prepare your mind.

For example, if you had a strong commitment to developing six pack abs from the gym, wouldn't you think you would gain the greatest results by bringing a specifically designed "Six Pack Ab" workout plan to the gym with you? Of course.

Preparing your mind is no different than your ab muscles, and if not trained or exercised, will become weak and useless. With consistent effort and focus, you will be able to develop your mind to the point where you could be diagnosed with a serious illness and respond with, "Well, I can't change it now. What is the first step to fixing the problem from where we are at now?" In that statement, you are able to act and NOT react.

> "By failing to prepare,
> you are preparing to fail."
>
> — Benjamin Franklin

In the final step, you will feel fatigue. This is the push back you will receive from your Negative Attitude, as they will try to use behaviors that drain your energy. Just like any person you have ever met that is in shape will tell you, it isn't easy when you first get started. However, by consistently going to the gym, things become easier each day. Just as muscle develops with routine exercise, your mind and Positive Warriors will also gain strength and endurance.

However, if you feel as though you are hitting a "wall" or plateauing in life, this is the point where you need to start breaking down the walls of your limiting beliefs. This wall is the maximum capacity that your Positive Attitude can muster, as it isn't developed enough to become great. You must have the courage to bust that wall and recognize that your "Attitudinal Why" is waiting for you on the other side. I promise this is going to be difficult. We find it hard to take responsibility for everything (especially when things go wrong). We create our own lives through our thoughts, actions, and words!

As I mentioned to you in the beginning, Fear is the one key warrior that isn't talked about as much as it needs to be. This warrior never wants to be exposed, and will typically hid in the back of the battleground. Yet, he will have the audacity to chant commands to the front lines to protect himself from the daily fight. He is a coward, afraid, and timid. However if not captured and defeated by the Positive Attitude he will play a major role in the outcome of your mental battleground.

Fear loves control and self-doubt. Primarily, the only way that Fear will prosper and develop is from enough drama, judgments, and resistance. If it isn't fought off or confronted soon enough, you'll always be left wondering where your freedom went in your life. Fear is likely to infiltrate through your thoughts, actions, and body language.

"Fear is only as deep
as the mind allows."

-Japanese Proverb

This is an ugly monster that isn't going to be easy to defeat. He will make you create drama, fill your mind with doubt, and destroy your confidence. Elect Freedom as your Positive Attitude warrior here. This is why it is so critically important to have a well-defined vision and goals. Don't allow your vision and goals to be cast away in the fog of life. Your reasons for success need to be strong and defined. If they are not, fear will find out and destroy everything you have worked so hard for up until now.

Freedom is a Positive Attitude warrior that is strong enough to break the shackles fear keeps on your mind, preventing growth and expansion. Use this warrior to omit your fear by sharing with fear your reasons, your vision, and your "Attitudinal Why" on a daily basis.

I challenge you to take freedom to the mental gym every day. Give it a chance to grow and develop. Allow it to grow by you writing your goals down before you go to bed and when you get up in the morning.

I encourage you to, please, stop living with the mindset that you can only be rich someday if you win the lottery or inherit a bunch of money. I promise you, things will NEVER change when you choose to retain that train of thought.

The final step was designed to give you the final tools you'll need to have consistent victories over Negative Attitude. You have now learned how important it is to be aware of a situation or pre-existing belief before you can change anything.

The ability to be able to act on a situation, rather than react, will potentially serve as one of the greatest tools you'll have taken from this book when applied to your world.

Simply by spending a few minutes each night thinking about some of the situations you might deal with the next day (both good and bad situations) will put you in a far more prepared mental position.

Follow the old saying, "Expect the best, and prepare for the worst".

I promise you, the people that show up to work on the day a project is due and it isn't complete will say, "Gosh, I never saw that coming!" They didn't spend enough time preparing for the next day the night prior. Remember, to act and not react comes through time and preparation.

Action: In the final step, step 8, the primary focus is taking responsibility for everything that has and will happen in your life.

- Grab another sheet of paper if necessary...

- Take a moment to think about what you have going on tomorrow. Write down a potential conversation you're going to have, or a billing issue you'll have to face.

✓ Using that, write down what choices you will make if everything goes perfect in your conversation and billing issue. Then, write down how you will prepare your Positive Attitude to fight back if everything goes backwards in the conversations tomorrow.

✓ This should only take a moment. Take your cell phone and set a timer for 5 minutes. This will allow you to stay focused in the completion of the final step of this program!

List a few situations that might arise in your day tomorrow.

1. *"I am making the choice to talk to Beth tomorrow about her performance at work."*

2. *"I am making the choice to talk with Paul about a billing issue we've had when dealing with his company."*

What will you do to prepare yourself for the potential situations you'll deal with tomorrow?

1. *The positive situation will be finding a mutual agreement on the work program we will implement for her. A negative situation would be her walking out. If that should happen, I will be prepared to*

acknowledge her frustrations and find common ground.

2. *The positive situation will be finding a mutual agreement of when to pay his bills moving forward. A negative situation would be Paul deciding to place his business with another company. If this should happen, I will be prepared to acknowledge his frustrations, and offer a new payment option to save the account.*

CONCLUSION

You did it! Congratulations! I'm very proud of the fact you were willing to invest the time to read this book. I have such an appreciation for your time, as it is something that you can never get back (in my mind I place a higher value on that than money). I have no doubt that your investment will pay off. It is up to you, however, to create the type of results you have always been desiring.

What I hope you have taken away after reading this book is an acknowledgement that you should always seek to find a better you. Take the time to really analyze your life choices up until this point, and try take a moment to reflect on how you have impacted those around you. Consider your understanding of who your friends are, what individual strengths and resources they offer, and how you can leverage their strengths to create a better version of you. On the flip side, you were also challenged to take a close look at some of the friends you have held on to for too long.

A couple items I want you to consider walking away are:

- What action will I take tomorrow to create a better attitude?

- Who are the negative people or thoughts I need to eliminate to get on the right track to overhauling my attitude?

Challenge yourself, take a look at your calendar, and set aside 15 minutes to have a meeting with yourself. In such a fast paced world, you might forget the knowledge you've gained from this book if you're not able to put it into immediate action. During that 15 minutes, identify the negative people in your life. You can never truly make a change unless you are willing to state whom or what is the problem keeping yourself from achieving your true potential.

If you make the choice to take no action and not make the commitment, you will have to live with your results. You will have to live with settling for a life that had so much more potential. You will have to live with the consequences of being mediocre your entire life. At this point forward you can't claim ignorance or say, "I didn't know" as an excuse to become less than you ought to be.

This officially marks the beginning of your journey overhauling your individual attitude. I look forward to hearing about your results!

For more information about this book and so much more, visit me at www.kylezdroik.com

Made in the USA
Monee, IL
10 December 2021

84635545R00075